Cycle of Rice
Cycle of Life

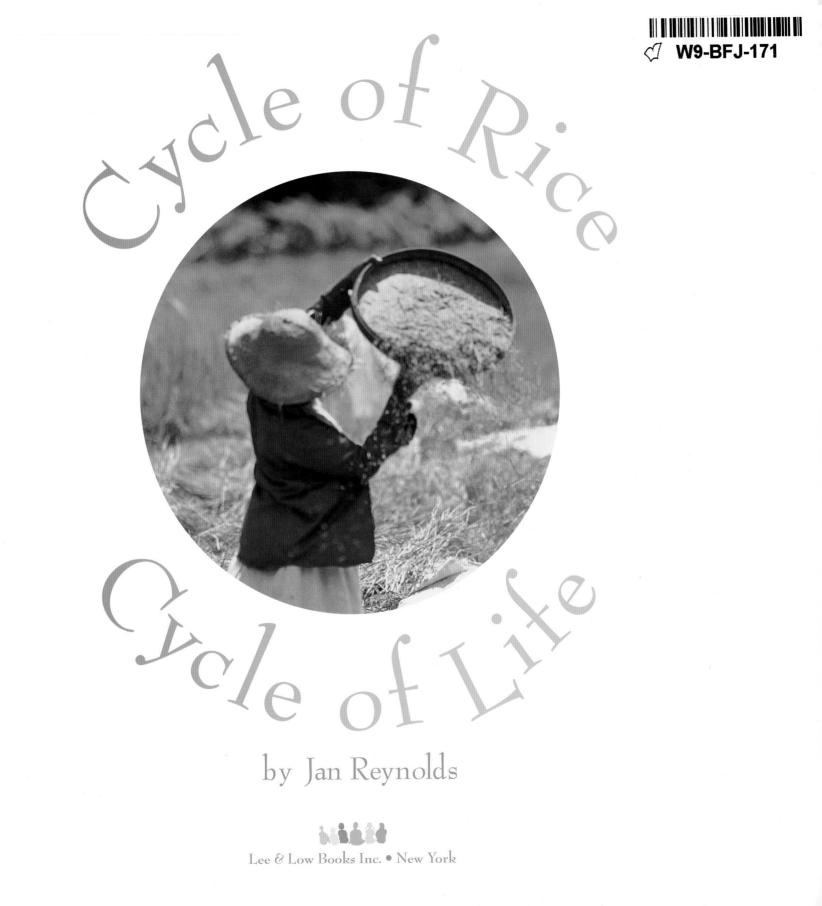

by Jan Reynolds

Lee & Low Books Inc. • New York

To Professor Stephen Lansing, for shining your spirit of goodwill my way, allowing me to experience your rich cultural world and valuable environmental work on the island of Bali. Your efforts are an inspiration to us all—J.R.

Acknowledgments
Special thanks to the Lintilhac Foundation for sending me to Bali, the James Robison Foundation for its assistance with the Rice Web book development, and the National Science Foundation for its work supporting scientists.

Sources
Much of the research for this book came from the author's fieldwork and primary observations while in Bali, as well as ongoing conversations with Professor J. Stephen Lansing.

Additional Sources
Eisman, Fred B., Jr. *Bali: Sekala and Niskala*; Essays on Religion, Ritual, and Art.
    Hong Kong: Periplus Editions, 1990.
Greenway, Paul, James Lyon, and Tony Wheeler. *Bali and Lombok: Island Dharma and Kuta Karma*.
    Oakland, CA: Lonely Planet, 1999.
Lansing, J. Stephen. *Priests and Programmers*.
    Princeton, NJ: Princeton University Press, 1991.

Manufactured in China by Jade Productions

Book design by Cohava Dodo
Book production by The Kids at Our House

The text is set in ITC Caslon 224 and Bernhard Modern

(HC) 10 9 8 7 6 5 4 3 2 1
(PB) 10 9 8
First Edition

Library of Congress Cataloging-in-Publication Data
Reynolds, Jan.
Cycle of rice, cycle of life : a story of sustainable farming / by Jan Reynolds. — 1st. ed.
            p. cm.
        Summary: "Photo-essay exploring the cultural and environmental aspects of traditional Balinese rice farming, a model of sustainable food production. Includes a map, foreword, and author's note."—Provided by publisher.
        ISBN 978-1-60060-254-2 (hardcover)   ISBN 978-1-62014-078-9 (paperback)
1. Rice—Indonesia—Bali Island—Pictorial works—Juvenile literature. 2. Sustainable agriculture—Indonesia—Bali Island—Pictorial works—Juvenile literature. I. Title.
SB191.R5R49 2009
633.1'80959862—dc22   2008030518

Foreword

A food staple for half the planet's population, rice is one of the most important crops on Earth. It is at the core of daily life and culture in many parts of the world.

To the people living on the small Indonesian island of Bali, rice is life. All the cycles of life are coordinated with the cycles of rice farming—the water cycle and the growing cycle. The island's rich volcanic soil, warm climate, and abundant moisture allow for one of the most productive rice harvests in the world.

There is also another reason for the Balinese's success. When it comes to growing rice, they have developed one of the world's most efficient systems for water sharing, crop rotation, and the use of natural fertilizers and pest control. Traditional Balinese rice farming is a dynamic model of sustainable farming, a way to grow food while being conscious of the needs of other people and the well-being of the planet.

a gift from the goddess

The Cycle of Water

High atop a mountain ridge on the island of Bali sits a glorious temple, *Ulun Danu Batur*. Open to the sky and the rains and the heavens above, it was built to honor *Dewi Danu*, a goddess of water. Like people everywhere, the Balinese know they cannot survive without water. It is essential for all life and sacred to their culture. Because of this, the Balinese have built temples such as Ulun Danu Batur to give thanks to Dewi Danu for blessing them with pure, life-giving water.

Bali is surrounded by water. Bordered by the Bali Sea to the north and the Indian Ocean to the south, it is one of more than 17,000 islands that make up the country of Indonesia in Southeast Asia. The salty seawater surrounding Bali cannot be used for farming, since crops require freshwater to grow. For freshwater, farmers must rely on rain that first falls on the island's highest peaks—volcanoes as tall as 10,000 feet (3,048 meters) that shape the backbone of Bali. Near volcanic mountains, such as Mount Batur, rain fills crater lakes that feed the island's eighty rivers. From the highest points on the island to the lowest, an ancient, elaborate water system flows down the hillsides, through the plains, and out to the ocean.

Although Bali's lakes and rivers exist naturally, a human-made marvel of hydro engineering has harnessed these waters for more than a thousand years. An interlocking network of tunneled waterways weaves its way through every bit of land on the island, providing residents with freshwater.

The water system was built by hand in the ninth century, using only what nature provided: earth, logs, and stone. Today some structures have been replaced, or expanded with cement and other modern materials, but much of the original framework remains. Weirs, or diversionary dams, change the natural flow of water so it runs in other directions. Tunnels angling slightly downhill and canals, human-made streams, transport water from high mountainsides to lower ground. Aqueducts carry water across busy travel routes and other obstacles. Finally, long irrigation ditches bring the water right into farmers' fields.

Water Temple System

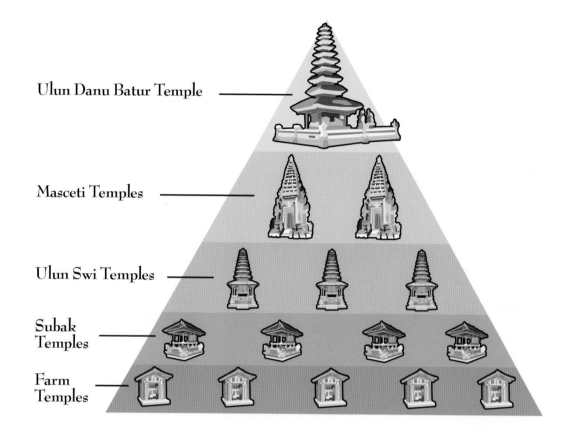

Ulun Danu Batur Temple

Masceti Temples

Ulun Swi Temples

Subak Temples

Farm Temples

Built along this intricate water system like beads on a necklace is a linked network of temples where water ceremonies take place. The holiest of temples, Ulun Danu Batur, sits at the top of this chain above the crater lake, Batur. Fanning out below Ulun Danu Batur are the *Masceti* temples. These large temples sit above entire farming regions. Weirs direct water from multiple rivers to form a region's communal water system. Below the Masceti temples are the *Ulun Swi* temples, which connect with a single weir, canal, or spring. The water from the Ulun Swi temples supplies many *subaks*, or groups of farms. There is also a separate temple for each subak, as well as a smaller temple for every individual farm. In this way, all points along this linked system of water sharing have their own corresponding water temples.

woman worshiping at farm temple in field

The *Jero Gde*, or high priest, a most respected man, blesses drops of holy water gathered from the steamy vents near the summit of Batur volcano. This is the most sacred ceremony, taking place at Ulun Danu Batur. After adding other water to the sacred drops, the Jero Gde will distribute holy water to visitors who come to the temple seeking it. Visitors take the holy water back to their communities for local water ceremonies and celebrations giving thanks to the water goddess. These rituals are all part of *Agama Tirtha*, honoring the gift of water.

temple offerings

Whoever offers to me with devotion,
a leaf, a flower, a fruit, or water,
with a pure heart, I accept.
— *the Bhagavad Gita*

Rituals performed at the water temples serve many purposes. Besides offering thanks and asking for plenty of water and good crops, these rituals connect people living in one watershed, or area united by a common water source. Gathering together as a community reminds them that others depend on the water too. It is important that every farming family within each subak has enough fresh water to grow the rice they need to feed themselves. Since farmers must visit and place offerings at temples along each part of the waterway, the rituals also help to ensure proper supervision and maintenance of the entire water system.

Like the Chinese *yin* and *yang*,
kaja-kelod, "toward the mountains–toward the sea,"
is the Balinese concept of balance in nature, encompassing
up and down, high and low, sacred and unholy.

Water that began as rainfall on Batur volcano eventually winds its way down to the shore of the Indian Ocean and the Tanah Lot temple. Here freshwater streams enter salty ocean water. Looking beyond Tanah Lot to the vast horizon, it is possible to see great clouds formed by evaporating water blowing toward the mountains. The clouds will release the water, raining down on Batur volcano and Ulun Danu Batur temple, and again the water will flow throughout Bali and back out to the ocean. This perfect natural cycle of water is sacred to all Balinese people. It is honored daily through temple offerings and the spirit of a connected community sharing water to insure a good life for all.

a time to grow

The Cycle of Rice

Parades of brightly dressed people carrying plates of luscious fruit and flower offerings on their heads follow priests in pure white sarongs as they walk to the temple for the planting celebration. This is the time, before each planting season, when representatives from the subaks come together at the Masceti temples at the heads of their watersheds. For hundreds of years these ritual gatherings have linked all the people in the watershed, uniting them to celebrate and share the natural gifts of their island home.

Gatherings at the Masceti temples are beautiful and rich in cultural tradition, but they are also a time for business. New irrigation projects are approved, disputes are settled, and advice is given for construction and repairs to fields and the water system. Most importantly, the farmers who are representing their subaks must work together to devise the best water-sharing schedule for the hundreds of people on the numerous farms within their watershed. The water will flow downhill from subak to subak through canals with dividers to control the agreed upon flow. Made up of emerald green terraced fields, the subaks are engineered like stair steps, creating flat spaces on the hillsides to pool the water for growing rice.

Developing water schedules requires complicated planning and organization. Everyone's needs must be considered in order to maximize the rice yield and benefit the common good. If disputes arise, they are settled by temple priests. When the meetings are finished, subak representatives send word to individual farming families within their watershed telling them when they will be receiving water for their fields.

As water flows through each subak, it is shared among the individual farms. The first stage of rice growth demands the most water, and a farmer upstream will typically let the water flow from his fields to his neighbor's two to four weeks after his own fields have been planted.

On one farm, a boy named Putu and his family will soon receive the water in their fields. Putu and his sister, Kadek, take offerings to the rice goddess *Dewi Sri* at a field temple.

Meanwhile, their grandfather has been aerating the fields, loosening the soil so that air can get below the surface. This is done with plows pulled by water buffalo or by hand with rakes. When the water comes, it flows into the field, flooding it about 1 to 2 feet (30 to 60 centimeters).

For two weeks prior to the flooding, rice seeds at the edge of the field have been sprouting into green shoots. They are now about 5 to 10 inches (13 to 25 centimeters) high and ready for Grandfather to plant in the flooded field. Planting the shoots is precise work and must be done by hand.

Long narrow pathways of dirt and grass rise up out of the water, crisscrossing the newly planted rice fields. These pathways are repaired and rebuilt every planting season so that people can travel throughout the wet fields. The pathways also enable young people such as Putu and Kadek to catch the frogs, eels, and small fish that can be found in the water.

As the rice grows taller and sprouts more stalks, small, sweet kernels form on the tips of the plants. These kernels will ripen and harden to become rice. Putu and Kadek must ward off the birds and protect their crop. They make scarecrows by tying strings and rags onto long bamboo sticks and placing them around the field.

Two to four months into the growing cycle, the rice plants have matured, reaching shoulder height for Putu and Kadek, approximately 4 feet (122 centimeters). After giving thanks to Dewi Sri for this wonderful crop of rice, the children are ready to help with the harvest. With his traditional curved knife, Putu is swift at cutting through the thick bundles of stalks.

Kadek strikes harvested stalks against the side of a basket. This knocks off the kernels of rice, which are collected in the basket below. The rice kernels will then be tossed in large, round sieves to separate out any small pieces of stalk or other materials. Finally, the rice will be laid in the sun to dry thoroughly, before it is packed into bags.

In Bali there are three separate words for rice:
padi when it is in the field
beras when it is dried, uncooked
nasi when it is cooked

After all the rice is harvested and the field is completely cut, the stalks are left to rot and break down in a small amount of remaining water. They will decompose, returning to the soil and making it rich in nutrients and healthy enough to grow the next crop of rice. This is the cycle of rice: circling from seeds to rice-bearing plants to cut stalks that go back into the soil.

Can the Cycle Continue?

After the harvest, the field is fallow, or without crops, but there is still work to be done. Putu waves a long bamboo pole to herd his family's ducks to the spot where he wants them to settle down and eat. He must guess which way the ducks might run and head them off. Duck herding is a lively game, but it is also an important job. The ducks play a crucial role in allowing the cycle of rice to continue, year after year, for generations to come.

When only one type of crop is planted over and over in the same soil, the soil often becomes depleted of certain nutrients and eventually loses the ability to support another planting of the same crop. Maintaining fertile soil is one of the most difficult problems facing farmers around the world. Another major problem is getting rid of pests such as insects and animals that eat their crops.

On farms in Bali, ducks work as natural pesticides and fertilizers for the rice fields. When Putu herds the ducks around the freshly cut field after the growing cycle, the ducks eat worms and bugs. If these pests were not controlled, they could multiply to great numbers on leftover rice kernels. By the following planting season, this increased number of pests could cause damage to the next crop of rice.

After eating pests, ducks digest this food and deposit manure, which then decomposes. Along with any decomposing leftover rice stalks, duck manure fertilizes the soil, making it healthy for the next crop of rice plants.

Because of the ducks, the fields are cleared of harmful pests and the soil is fortified with nutrients. This type of rice farming is a form of *sustainable agriculture*, which means the crop can be grown over and over on the same land, year after year. Since this type of farming does not use chemicals that could be harmful to the land, air, and water, the system is also *environmentally sustainable*. It causes no lasting damage to the earth.

Although this traditional Balinese method of rice farming has been successful for more than a thousand years, in the 1960s something unusual happened. Because Bali was the best rice producer out of the thousands of islands that make up Indonesia, the government decided that it would make Bali an even better rice producer. The extra rice would then be used to help feed the country's growing population. The government agreed to participate in an international program called the Green Revolution. This program promoted the planting of hybrid rice, or rice modified in a laboratory that could grow to maturity more quickly than unmodified rice.

Instead of following their usual patterns of the growing cycle—alternating between planting fields and leaving them fallow—Balinese farmers were asked to plant as much hybrid rice as they could as often as they could. The government spent millions of dollars building new dams and irrigation systems to support this continuous rice planting. The ceremonial organization of water-sharing schedules among the farmers was eliminated. This threw the ancient water temple system into chaos, threatening the ties that had connected community members and synchronized their lives with the natural cycles of water and plants.

The big surprise was that the best rice producer in Indonesia soon became the worst. Bali's rice productivity decreased sharply because the fields were in use continuously. There was never a fallow period, so rice stalks could not decompose back into the soil and ducks were not able to scavenge. The overused soil became depleted of nutrients. Pests overran the fields, devouring rice before it could be harvested.

More and more chemical fertilizers and pesticides had to be used to replace lost nutrients in the soil and control the increasing numbers of pests. Instead of fixing these problems, however, the chemicals caused more damage. Many were toxic and ran into the water system and out to the ocean, damaging water-dwelling life and harming the coral reefs. The chemicals even ended up in the water that people drank. In addition, the pesticides were not effective in killing the pests. The result was stronger, more chemically resistant strains of pests.

Within a few years it became evident that the imposed system of the Green Revolution, with its fast-growing hybrid rice, was a disaster. The system decreased the very rice production it was meant to boost. This type of chemically enhanced agriculture was not sustainable. It could not maintain healthy, abundant crops of rice year after year, even with the aid of chemical pesticides and fertilizers. Worst of all, the new system was dangerous to the environment and people of Bali.

chemical fertilizers and pesticides

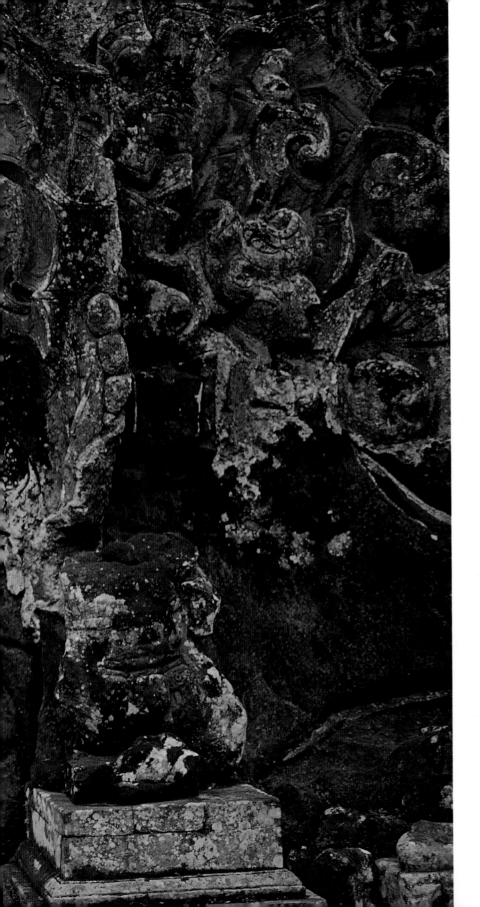

tradition vs. technology

Saving the Cycle

During the time of the Green Revolution, J. Stephen Lansing, an American anthropologist from the University of Southern California, was spending time in Bali studying the water temple system. Lansing became aware that the Jero Gde, other priests, and farmers in the temple system all played significant roles in the intricate structure of Balinese rice farming. He also realized that this traditional system took into account important aspects of ecology and social networking. Now this centuries-old system was under serious threat from the new hybrid rice planting. Lansing knew something had to be done. He set out to help restore the traditional Balinese rice-farming practices before the land and system were damaged forever.

For more than a thousand years, sacred water ceremonies were led by the priests and Jero Gde. Water was shared and the community was united. Rice crops were abundant and the people and land were cared for. It was a synchronized system that worked in perfect harmony.

J. Stephen Lansing

Lansing saw the social, environmental, and agricultural value in this traditional, sustainable method of rice farming. He sought a way to explain to the Indonesian government that hybrid rice and chemicals were not the answer to producing large crops. Government officials needed to understand that the water temple system was essential to Bali's production of abundant rice crops and to protecting the land. But the government did not want to listen. They sent Lansing reports from civil engineers saying, "The [farmers] don't need a high priest. They need a hydrologist [water scientist]." Letters from officials claimed that the priests did not "exercise any active role in irrigation activities."

Frustrated but determined, Lansing returned to the United States. After obtaining a National Science Foundation grant, he enlisted the help of his friend, professor and ecologist James Kremer. Kremer traveled to Bali with Lansing. He hoped to learn about the ecosystem of the rice fields and the creatures living within it alongside Lansing's study of the water temple culture. What Kremer discovered was that *pulsing systems* were more productive than *static systems*. This meant rice fields produced more when water flowed in and out of the fields—allowing for a fallow period in between growing cycles—than if the fields were kept flooded continually. Pulsing also cut down on the number of pests because of the fallow, duck-scavenging periods between floodings.

rice fields in different stages of growth

To Lansing and Kremer, the ancient water temple system of farming seemed to be more productive from a cultural and ecological point of view. Now they had to convince the Indonesian government of this. They decided to put together a computerized model of the data they had gathered. The program calculated potential harvests under any given conditions by incorporating all the variables in rice farming, such as rainfall, planting schedules, and pest proliferation. The computer was like a crystal ball, making predictions. In many ways it did what the priests and farmers had been doing for more than a thousand years. What the farmers traditionally prayed for to the goddesses Dewi Danu of water and Dewi Sri of rice could be replicated on a computer screen.

Lansing did not want the computer model to replace the traditional system of farmers and priests. Instead, he hoped it would help them. He thought they might be able to use it in conjunction with their own predictions and decision making. More importantly, he wanted the computer model to demonstrate to members of the Indonesian government just how much work the farmers and priests had been doing all along. Lansing met with government officials to show them the model. Seeing all the variables that had to be predicted for successful crops, the government officials began to understand the valuable and complicated job priests and farmers had managed. They realized the temple system had coordinated water sharing and crop rotation better than the government had.

The water temple system was reinstated for the majority of farms across Bali. Farmers returned to the old rituals of crop planting and water sharing. Productivity increased and the need for pesticides declined sharply, as fields were once again allowed to lie fallow. However, some lasting effects of the Green Revolution remained. Because the chemical balance of the soil had been disrupted, many farmers still had to use chemical fertilizers. This posed a continued threat to the environment.

government official studying computer model

Let us think of the lovely splendor of the God of the sun that he may inspire our minds.
—the Gayatri Mantra

Stephen Lansing's work prompted a wide-ranging effort in Bali and other parts of the world to evaluate traditional ways of farming before imposing modern techniques. His work showed that blending the old and new—ancient tradition with cutting-edge technology—can promote unique ways of thinking about our global future. Computer models such as Lansing and Kremer's are now being used to explore sustainable agriculture in different parts of the world. Other environmental issues such as deforestation and the impact of global warming are being studied with these kinds of models too.

Lansing continues his work in Bali. With the water temple system restored, he is leading a campaign to reduce the lingering use of chemical fertilizers. He hopes one day to see Bali return completely to the traditional, chemical-free methods of farming that worked so well for centuries.

Balinese farmers know their lives must be lived in harmony with natural cycles in order to carry on their rice farming for the next thousand years. They have a special prayer, *Om sarwa prani hitangkaram*—"May all that breathes be well." If the natural world is in balance, then all is in harmony on the island of Bali. Life can be sustainable, and children such as Putu and Kadek can imagine a future of hope for themselves and generations to come.

As palm and banana trees sway in the breeze at dusk, coconut shells float like little boats, carrying the day's offerings of rice pastry and flowers down the river. The Tanah Lot temple is silhouetted against the darkening sky near where these offerings will flow out into the vast ocean. Once again water will evaporate into the clouds and rain down into Lake Batur, perhaps becoming precious drops of holy water. Once again there will be a celebration at every water temple, every rice harvest, and every home, honoring the cycle of water, the cycle of rice, and the cycle of life on the beautiful island of Bali.

Author's Note

Balinese rice farmers spend their days in the natural world, in sync with the cycles of the water, land, and air. They know water evaporates from the sea into the clouds and comes back down as rain. They know plants grow and die, returning to the soil to make it fertile for new plants. They know the air they breathe is shared with the plants they grow and all life on Earth.

In industrial societies such as the United States, much of the food is produced in factories and on large commercial farms that use potentially harmful chemicals. People can buy what they want at grocery stores or supermarkets quite easily without knowing how it was grown or raised. They are often unaware of the natural cycles of life that produce the foods that are available for purchase. Many people buy more than they need, and the excess gets thrown away. America's estimated food waste is an astounding 30 million tons (27 million metric tons) a year, most of which ends up in landfills.[1] Chemical pesticides and fertilizers used in commercial farming also damage the land and change the texture of the soil, causing the topsoil to wash into rivers along with the chemicals.

By buying more than is needed, creating large amounts of trash, and producing harmful waste year after year, the water, land, and air are continually damaged. This is not a sustainable lifestyle. Eventually the earth won't be able to produce what people need to live, and natural cycles will break down. A sustainable world "meets the needs of the present, without compromising the ability of future generations to meet their own needs."[2] People must take care of the planet so it can provide for all of its inhabitants.

Around the world and in your own backyard, people are making important decisions every day to change the way they live. Organic vegetable and fruit farmers sell produce they grow without the use of toxic chemicals. Consumers are choosing to eat more of what they can buy locally, so food is transported shorter distances, which reduces fuel usage and pollution. Instead of sending food waste to landfills, individuals and restaurants alike are composting, or allowing food waste to decompose back into usable soil. Families are planting their own fruit and vegetable gardens. There are also programs in communities and schools to teach people where their food comes from or how to grow it themselves. Each small step makes a difference in keeping the world a beautiful, sustainable system *for everyone.*

—*Jan Reynolds*

---

[1] Martin, Andrew, "One Country's Table Scraps, Another Country's Meal." *New York Times*, May 18, 2008.
[2] World Commission on Environment and Development (WCED), "Our Common Future." New York: Oxford University Press, 1987.

Map of Bali

Bali is approximately:
90 miles (145 kilometers) long
48 miles (77 kilometers) wide
2,175 square miles
(5,632 square kilometers) total area

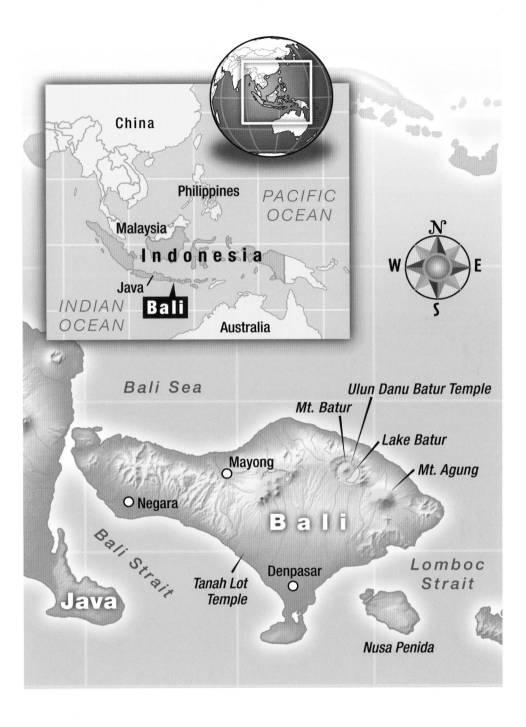

Web Sites

• Find out about food and hunger around the globe with the United Nations World Food Programme: **www.wfp.org**
• Play a fun vocabulary game while donating rice to countries in need: **www.freerice.com**
• Learn more about Professor J. Stephen Lansing's work: **www.slansing.org/Lansing_Website/Welcome.html**

Glossary/Pronunciation Guide

Variations in spelling and pronunciation of words may exist, particularly for Balinese words adapted into English.
Terms are defined in relation to the context of this book.

Agama Tirthu (ah-GAH-ma TER-thoo)—ritual honoring of water

aerate (AIR-ate)—to mix air into soil

aqueduct (AK-wuh-duhkt)—structure used to transport water over ground

Balinese (bah-leh-NEEZ)—of the island or people of Bali

Bali (bah-LEE)—island that is part of the country Indonesia

decompose (dee-kuhm-POZE)—to break down or decay

ecological (ek-uh-LOJ-i-kuhl)—relating to plants, animals, and the environment

Dewi Danu (DO-weh dah-NOO)—goddess of water or lakes

Dewi Sri (DO-weh sree)—goddess of rice

environmentally sustainable (en-VYE-ruhn-ment-ah-lee suh-STAYN-ah-buhl)—does not harm the environment over time

evaporate (eh-VAP-uh-rate)—to turn from liquid to gas

fallow (FAL-oh)—without crop; not planted

fertilizer (FUR-tuh-lize-er)—substance that puts nutrients in soil

hybrid (HYE-brid)—plant species altered by science

hydrologist (HYE-drah-loh-gist)—scientist who studies water

Indonesia (in-doh-NEE-zha)—country in Southeast Asia made up of more than 17,000 islands

Jero Gde (JEE-row geh-DAY)—high priest of water ceremonies

Kadek (KAH-deck)—girl's name

kaja-kelod (KAH-ja KEH-lahd)—Balinese saying meaning "toward the mountains-toward the sea;" represents balance in the natural world

Masceti (MAS-che-tee)—type of temple serving a large farming region united by multiple rivers

Om sarwa prani hitangkaram (om SAR-wah PRA-nih hi-TANG-ka-ram)—Balinese prayer meaning "May all that breathes be well."

pesticide (PESS-tuh-side)—substance that kills insects or other pests

proliferation (pruh-LIF-er-ay-shun)—increasing in numbers, or multiplying, of something

pulsing system (PUHLSS-ing SISS-tuhm)—farming system marked by change or movement; in this case, the flow of water into and out of the fields

Putu (POO-too)—boy's name

subak (SOO-bahk)—group of farms

sustainable agriculture (suh-STAYN-ah-buhl AG-ruh-kul-chur)—farming that can keep going over time without damage to land or crop yields

static system (STAT-ik SISS-tuhm)—farming system that does not change or move; in this case, water remaining in fields constantly, not flowing in or out

Taneh Lot (TAN-uh lot)—temple in Bali that overlooks the sea

Ulun Swi (OO-lun swee)—type of temple serving multiple subaks, or groups of farms

Ulun Danu Batur (OO-lun DAH-new BAH-toor)—temple in Bali near Batur volcano and crater lake

watershed (WAH-tur-shed)—area connected by a shared water source

weir (wihr *or* ware)—dam; structure to hold back water